W9-AHU-867

Celebrate
the Sun

OTHER BOOKS BY JAMES KAVANAUGH

A Modern Priest Looks at His Outdated Church

The Birth of God

There Are Men Too Gentle To Live Among Wolves

The Crooked Angel

Between Man and Woman

Will You Be My Friend?

Faces in the City

James Kavanaugh

Celebrate the Sun

A Sunrise Book

E. P. Dutton & Co., Inc., New York

Library of Congress Catalog Card Number: 72-95238
Standard Book Number: 0-87690-163-1

Printed in the United States of America.

10 9 8 7 6 5 4 3 2

to those who take time
to celebrate the sun
—and are grateful

———————————————————————

Celebrate
the Sun

There was every reason to believe that Harry Langendorf Pelican would make it big. Although he was hatched late in the season, the signs attending his birth were portentous and unique. He appeared on a small island off the coast of Mexico, June 21, the very day of the summer solstice, precisely at high noon. And although he was the smallest of the three eggs, his incubation period was only twenty-four days—as if he were impelled by an intense eagerness to be released from the shell. At only two weeks of age he startled everyone by climbing from the nest to explore the rugged volcanic rocks and the unfriendly cactus that covered the little island. He learned to fly quickly and soared quite gracefully at seven weeks.

He was a charming and affectionate bird as well. When the adult pelicans returned from the sea with a pouch full of mashed anchovies to feed their own squawking young, Harry Langendorf could wheedle choice mouthfuls from comparative strangers. When his own parents returned from fishing, he wagged his head in cute little ways, pecked tenderly at their bills, bowed gracefully and immersed his head in their giant pouches to feed. Then he fell comically to the ground, whirled around in grateful circles and opened his bill in his special broad smile.

His father, Charlie Langendorf, who had always been an obscure and extremely average pelican, was determined to transform his talented son into an island prodigy. Previously, Charlie had known only great misfortune with his offspring. Two years in a row, the eggs of his mate had been too thin-shelled to hatch. One year, the gulls had maneuvered him from the nest while his mate was fishing and the screaming pirates had devoured the eggs. Another year, a young son had crashed into the rocks while soloing and another had died tragically while demanding food from a cactus which he mistook for Charlie.

Even the amazing Harry Langendorf had been born late in the mating season because Charlie had delayed the building of his nest and had almost been left without a mate. And when the mate appeared, a wandering stranger, she was too clumsy and big-boned to attract anything but criticism and snide comments. Some of her mannerisms indicated that she might have come from the Galápagos Islands far to the south, but most of the prominent females considered her far too awkward to manage such a flight. She herself said nothing.

Wherever she came from, she had given Charlie the son he had dreamed about, and his pride was profound. Everywhere there was talk of his talented son, and Charlie hovered over him week after week, from morning till night, pushing him to excel. Harry Langendorf began to fish for himself when his brother and sister were barely able to fly and, as the months passed and he grew more mature, it was not unusual to see him leading other pelicans across the waves, scaling over crests and into valleys, rising high with the wind to dive for the deeper fish. He learned to lower his bill with confidence, to set his wings with precision when he plummeted in for the kill. After long hours of practice, he learned to hit the water without fear, to make a graceful somersault under the waves, to surface and lower his pouch for the water to drain out. Then he raised his bill to swallow the fish and took off into the wind with powerful strokes of his webbed feet. And as the weeks flew by, the wily gulls who waited to snatch fish from the more awkward pelicans soon proved no match for the speed and skill of Harry Langendorf.

He learned to watch the gulls and shearwaters to find the fish and to wait for the sea lions to drive the fish to the surface. He never pursued the fishing boats for garbage, like the gulls and cormorants, and shied away from the piers where the fishermen caught unsuspecting pelicans in their lines and lead weights, and beat them to death with wooden clubs.

And how he could fly, soaring and scaling, plummeting and gliding, and winging his way across the sea. He flew to exceptional heights, took exciting trips along the coast of California to Oregon and Washington and the waters of Vancouver. He flew south beyond Baja and along the coasts of Mexico, sampling the sardines and anchovies and small sea bass as he went. Often he traveled alone or with only a few friends since most of the other pelicans were content to remain within fifty or a hundred miles from home. And Charlie pushed and prodded him without restraint. Nothing Harry Langendorf did was ever enough, and the gentle, quiet reassurances of his mother were smothered by the noisy goading of Charlie.

Soon she had little to say and was largely ignored by the colony. No one knew anything about her. The very fact that she would mate with Charlie was evidence of her tawdriness. Besides, she seemed silent and aloof, molted quite distastefully, and had not a single friend on the island. Most of the females resented her from the very beginning when she, an awkward stranger, produced three healthy eggs. She didn't seem to mind the unkindness, however, and spent endless

hours watching the waves and the playful sea lions and the boisterous fishermen who shouted at her as they passed nearby.

Harry Langendorf loved her deeply and enjoyed the special moments when they sat together and watched the sun set splendidly in the distance. She shared some secret communion with the sun and her eyes assumed a gentle glow at its rising and setting. It was as if some mystic energy took possession of her and she longed to share it with Harry Langendorf. At such moments they scarcely uttered a word, but there was some deep and unspoken bond between them.

Charlie, however, gave them little time together and dragged Harry Langendorf off to practice his free falls and power dives or to drive him to record heights above the mountains and the clouds. As he grew older, his training for long-distance flights obliged him to spend increasing periods of time away from the island. He was gone for weeks at a time and, one day, when he was racing somewhere along the coasts of Northern California, his mother disappeared from the island and was never seen again.

When Harry Langendorf returned, she was gone. He was grief-stricken for several weeks and spent most of his time alone, angry at himself for having ignored her, angry at Charlie and the island colony for not having accepted her. When the females offered their sympathy, he raised his head and opened his inflated pouch in resentment, then flew away to the ancient reef along the coast where the old pelicans went to die. There, among the bones of the dead and the groans of the dying, the old, and the infirm, he watched the waves crashing against the rocks, studied the frolicking porpoises, and lost himself in the splendor of the setting sun.

On foggy days he flew out to sea, circled and scaled for hours on end. Then he rested on the water, drew his head into his shoulders as if to sleep, only to fly again to great heights and soar gracefully through the fog. He loved the season of the fog which softened the silhouette of the mountains and made serene the power of the sea. At night he stayed in secret spots along the coast, nestled among the rocks and small bushes and stared out at the silent water which trembled in the sinister light of the moon.

For days on end he sat motionless, lost in the panorama of the sunset filtering its dying light across the sky and transforming the white clouds into mountain peaks of pink and orange marble. Gradually, his grief faded and he could enjoy the memory of his mother, her soft and eloquent eyes, her serenity and strength in the face of misunderstanding, her silence when words were too feeble to capture beauty or to depict pain.

And then, one day, his weeks of grief were over and he knew it was time to return to the colony. He had missed his friends, missed their words of praise, missed the fishing trips along the coast. Harry Langendorf had become the pride of the colony and the pelicans flocked to welcome him and bowed to him in respect and admiration. His face seemed harder somehow, his bill more determined, his eyes colder and more distant. He was not a child anymore; the white of his under-belly was now streaked with a greyish brown and silver-grey feathers were beginning to appear on his back and wings and shoulders. His head was showing white and the feathers be-hind his neck were changing to a dark brown. Harry Langen-dorf Pelican was becoming a man.

For a few days he did not seem eager to drive himself as before. Charlie approached him: "You're not the same, Harry Langendorf. People are beginning to talk. You have an incredi-ble talent and you must use it."

Harry Langendorf stared at him coldly. "I do not need you," he said. The elders came to him: "We need your strength and vision, Harry Langendorf. You have a great responsibility be-cause you have given us great hope. Now we know what our destiny can be."

Again he stared coldly, but said nothing.

He needed a little more time to make life on the island seem real. He had retreated deep within himself during his weeks on the reef of the dead and felt as well the struggle of the pas-sage from boyhood to young manhood. For a time there was too much activity on the island for him to endure, too much motion to permit him peace. He stood apart and listened to the squawking of the young, heard the monotonous screams of the gulls and watched his friends struggle to understand the wind and the sea. Gradually he became more interested in life around him.

Then, quite suddenly one morning, he seemed to emerge from the shadows and silence and take his rightful place in the island colony with a more fierce determination than he had ever manifested before. With almost frenetic energy he led the fishing trips, frightened away the gulls with his pouch stretched open and his head flashing upwards at the sky. He snatched fish from the cormorants feeding on the surface, tossed a few scraps to mock the waiting gulls and amuse his admiring friends. Then he led them away, laughing, high above the water and soared gracefully back to the island. He was Harry Langendorf of old and more.

He spent his days teaching the young, showing them how to balance themselves on uneasy perches by flicking motions of their tails. He taught them to play dead, to scale up and down the waves, to spot the unhealthy fish which produced thin-shelled eggs. He improved their takeoffs, took them higher than they had ever been before and told them about the quiet lagoons far to the south where the fish were always sweet and healthy. He talked of the bays and rugged islands of the north.

No one could fly as fast as Harry Langendorf, nor climb as high. At times, he would lead the other birds into columnlike formations far above the mountains, or invade the bays along the California coastline, there to dive with such grace and power that the gulls stood silently along the shore in awe. Every day was a new challenge for him and nothing was too difficult to try. There had never been a pelican in thirty million years of history like the legendary Harry Langendorf Pelican.

And as the days passed, he grew more determined and intense. He did not laugh as much, there was no time to laugh, there were records to set and goals to reach. "You can lead us to the stars, Harry Langendorf," the pelicans said.

"Indeed I can—and I will," said Harry Langendorf. The pelicans bowed and wagged their heads, they raised and lowered their bills, preened their feathers, followed him in proud formation.

"We are not scavengers and pirates like the gulls," they said.

"Indeed, we are not," said Harry, "Nor are we clumsy like the cormorants or stupid like the shearwaters."

"No boobie or frigate bird alive can dive like Harry Langendorf," they said.

Harry Langendorf was truly happy. He had forgotten the sad days of mourning his mother. There was so much to live for, so much to be done. Every pelican in the colony was aware of him. The young came to him and talked of adventures on distant islands, of flying high above the clouds. Even the elders of the colony, some of whom wondered about him, approached with deep and ponderous considerations.

"You are pushing too hard, Harry Langendorf," they said.

"We cannot push too hard," he said. "We have been mediocre and foolish birds, filling our bellies and drifting aimlessly around, sitting lazily on sandbars until the changing tide forces us to move. We lose our eggs to the gulls and are content to smile and produce more."

"But we have been happy," they said.

"We have been foolish and unproductive," he said, "Limited and unimaginative. We have never reached beyond the clouds. This is one little island on one little sea. We have only begun to fly."

They were caught up in his words and his enthusiasm: "Will we outfly the eagle?" they asked. "Will we reach the moon?"

"I see no reason why not, if we strive mightily and discipline ourselves. We can do anything with faith," said Harry.

"Will we keep the gulls from stealing our eggs?" they asked.

"They will never steal any eggs of ours," he said, "Nor ever again peck out the brains of our children."

Never had there been such excitement in the colony, the young were more alive and exuberant, the adults more excited and in touch. They talked of new goals, new hopes, new strength. There were no limits, nothing would be denied them. Individual pelicans had never lived very long, although the species had survived for millions of years. Now there was talk of immortality. "Why should we die?" asked the old.

"There's no reason to," said Harry Langendorf. "You must have a goal, and when you complete that goal, you must have a higher one. You must never be satisfied. Satisfaction of any kind is death."

"We will not be satisfied, Harry Langendorf," they said. "Never!"

But some of the birds complained. "Why must we strive so hard?" they asked. "We have enjoyed our life, we have enjoyed our children. Sometimes our eggs are thin-shelled, sometimes there is tragedy and death, but we have known the sun and the sea, the soaring flights and the quiet vigils."

"It is not enough," said Harry Langendorf. "We are not admired. We are considered average, awkward, and simple. We have never flown as high as we are able, nor have we ever really pushed ourselves. We have been sluggish and aimless."

"But why should we strive? What is there to gain?"

"Life has no point unless you achieve greater things," said Harry Langendorf. "You simply live and die. That is not enough."

They were no match for his strength and eloquence. They waddled off along the rocks and stared out to sea.

It was early spring and the mating season would soon begin. The male birds were building their nests. They combed the area for branches and driftwood, bits of bronze kelp and dry bones, purple sea grass and soft feathers. The nests were built on the rocks or on the remains of former nests and were from five to ten inches high, and some reached two feet across. Harry Langendorf erected a beautiful nest, pulling the strong support twigs through the sides at the proper angle, his bill working like a giant needle.

When the foundation of the nest was ready, Harry Langendorf sat on it to await the approaching females who fought among themselves for a particularly attractive mate. They approached a nest, spotted the bowing and preening male they wanted and tried to move in. If he wanted her, he would hand her bits of material to complete the nest building. If he were disappointed, he would grab her neck and throw her from the nest. It was the time of high pelican passion.

Every female in the colony wanted to mate with Harry Langendorf, to bear his offspring, to know the power of his affection and unmatched protection. They did not, however, approach him boldly. It was rumored throughout the colony that Harry Langendorf had already decided on his mate. His father had talked to him, so had the elders. "You are special," they all said. "You must have someone worthy of you." And only Samantha Butterfield seemed right. She had the best blood in the colony; her father was a fifth-generation elder, her mother the granddaughter of the most respected sage on the island. There had been no thin-shelled eggs in her family even in the year of the great tragedy when only a few babies were born. Samantha was accustomed to greatness and had the mind and grace to deserve Harry Langendorf Pelican.

She approached him with confidence and good breeding, her bill upraised and her gular pouch inflated. She bowed to him, threw her head coyly, circled the nest, and pointed her bill with elegance and sophistication. Meanwhile Harry Langendorf bowed in turn and moved his bill excitedly around the nest. In the pelican tradition he did not overdo it. There was no strutting, no sexual display, no violent motion of the wings. Samantha Butterfield sensed his strength, his worried concern for the comfort and protection of the nest. He picked up a few strands of grass and handed them to her and she graciously wove them into the nest. She had been accepted and joined him in the love cottage while the entire colony held its breath.

Lovingly they worked together, alternately offering each other strands of grass or bits of twigs and weaving them into the nest. It was clear to the entire colony that they were meant for each other. And later in the afternoon, when the sun was like a giant orange-gold ball on the horizon, Harry Langendorf left the nest for a moment, circled it with his heavy, waddling walk, lifted his beak, moved his wings a bit and expanded his pouch mightily. Samantha Butterfield knew that this was the moment. She flattened her feathers, crouched low in the nest and waited. Her face was solemn and Harry Langendorf, with a like expression, joined her in the nest and mated with his

beloved. The love act was brief. She moved her wings with a slight flutter, trembled momentarily, then moved from the nest and flew solemnly down to the ocean. He followed her with dignity. They bathed carefully, beating their wings against the water, and lovingly sprayed water on one another. The entire colony was overjoyed.

Harry Langendorf was like a new man. He flew and fished with renewed and secret fury. No spouse ever had the security and comfort provided for Samantha. He had worried needlessly about the eggs since the two produced were firm-shelled and exceptionally large and a little brighter than the usually lusterless eggs of the pelican. And Harry Langendorf, the attentive husband, sought out the choicest fish for his bride, kept his eyes alert for the scavenging gulls, and took his turn standing on the nest to relieve Samantha. Using the ancient ceremony of nest-relief, he moved towards her with his bill almost straight up and his head waving from side to side. Samantha moved her wings gently in recognition, pointed her bill protectively into the nest and uttered a low, husky sound. Harry Langendorf continued to flash his bill back and forth like the conductor of a symphony. Then Samantha arose and Harry Langendorf climbed into the nest and wrapped his webbed feet carefully around the eggs. Samantha had time to bathe, to feed, to soar in celebration of her eggs and to rejoice in her perfect union with the unique and breathtaking Harry Langendorf Pelican.

There were the usual moments of anxiety, the passing fishermen who frightened some of the birds and caused them to crush their own eggs in the confusion, the marauding gulls who waited to snatch the unattended eggs. But whenever there was danger, Harry Langendorf was on the scene, his bill flashing like a saber, his pouch gaping fiercely. For the most part, life was serene. The summer days were warm and cloudless, the sea breeze soft and caressing, and the silent nights were clear and cool.

After a long month the chicks were hatched, formless masses of dark red skin with swollen little bumps for heads hanging down helplessly. The naked red skin gradually turned black in the sun, the eyes opened, and the babies stood up. Pinfeathers appeared after a week, then tufts of white down, and the first brown feathers in the middle of the third week.

At first it seemed easy for the parents to take care of them, to fill their pouches with regurgitated fish, force it to the tip of their bills, and offer it to the struggling babies. But after the fourth or fifth week the infant pelicans waddled from the nest and squawked their way among the other children swarming over the rocks. They pecked and pushed, clucked endlessly and shook their wings at every sound they made. They were discovering life, and when Harry Langendorf brought them morsels of soft fish, they had to fight their way through the crowd to find him. They pecked at his bill, squawked mercilessly, and stuck their heads into his pouch to be fed.

Soon they had to be taught to fly and fish and defend themselves against gulls. Samantha was insistent that they be exceptional and well-bred. They were not to be like other pelicans; they were a special breed and must strive and excel accordingly. Harry Langendorf was a masterful teacher and they learned quickly. Each new goal mastered meant that another one was set for them. The boy, Edward Langendorf, was exceptionally talented. He would be another prodigy in the colony, everyone knew it, the parents most of all. The girl, Mary Langendorf, was the image of her mother.

Harry Langendorf and Samantha Butterfield were demanding not only of themselves, but of their children as well. Edward and Mary were pushed and prodded to excel, to avoid the lazy pelicans who hung around the piers and stared vacantly out to sea. There were flying techniques to master, dives to perfect, takeoffs to improve, and distances to travel. Harry Langendorf watched the motion of their wings carefully, he criticized their somersaults in the water, and demanded that they never be satisfied.

"There must be no limits to our striving," he said. "With utter faith, all things are possible. The only boundaries are those that we set for ourselves."

He was equally hard on himself, flying above the clouds, improving his flight-in-fog ability, strengthening the power of his pouch, expanding it beyond normal limits. When he complained of weariness, Samantha was there to remind him that he was a pelican in pursuit of the highest goals.

Their days together as a family were times of constant activity and striving. There was hardly a chance to talk, to rest lazily on the rugged rocks of the island, to laugh at the sea lions playing follow-the-leader. Edward complained: "Why can't we enjoy ourselves like Michael Wilkie and Arthur Edwards? They can play on the rocks and float along the shore. They don't have to work so hard."

"You are different," said Harry Langendorf. "You must not waste time. You must not be mediocre."

"We are not ordinary pelicans," said Samantha Butterfield, "scrounging for food, staring at the waves, lumbering around the bays, scowling at the gulls. Someday you will thank us."

"We must continue to set ourselves new and higher goals," said Harry Langendorf. "We can be perfect pelicans, we only have to make the effort. Let the world know that we have passed through and conquered it."

Increasingly the driving spirit of Harry Langendorf affected the whole colony. He continued to be the charismatic and unquestioned leader. And for his followers, who formed a distant group of elitists, strength and power was supreme.

They thanked their forebears that they were not like the other pelicans, dirty and awkward, cowardly, wasteful, and downright lazy. They valued time and knew that only perfection of flight and power was important. They fished furiously, gulped down their food, and raced back into the sky to practice power dives and turns, new wing motions and smooth pull-outs. There was no time to chat with the old birds as before, no moments to watch the rising sun or the floating kelp knotting itself around the rocks and stretching on the sand to dry. The power of youth and strength was fostered, new goals were set, records were kept and honors were bestowed on the most accomplished and productive.

"I flew a hundred miles today, Harry Langendorf," said one.

"I flew a thousand miles this week," said another.

"I soared above the clouds today," said Warren Çovington, "and tomorrow I will go higher still. Soon, I will fly higher than Edward."

"I hardly have time to eat," said David McCarthy, "I am finally perfecting my dive."

Harry Langendorf was ecstatic. His spirit was capturing the young and lifting their ambitions to new heights. "We must keep active," he said. "Rest is for the weary and weak. We must be lean and tough, we must push and reach, search and strive, challenge and accomplish. Above all we must never be satisfied. Only perfection is enough."

At times Samantha Butterfield resented his prowess. She wanted to compete with him to keep his admiration and love. When she failed in a particular phase of flight, she feared that a more graceful pelican would steal him away. She watched the young with jealous eyes and criticized Harry Langendorf's accomplishments. He accepted her criticism as inspiration. "You are never satisfied," he said, "you never let me rest on my laurels."

Those who stood outside the elitist group were not admired. They were the old, the awkward, and meagerly talented, the fearful and handicapped, the silent dreamers. They spent their time leisurely, chatting and telling stories, fishing when they were hungry, staring out to sea and watching life around them. The young elitists avoided them because they had neither the strength nor the talent to compete and had nothing to contribute that the young considered important.

The outsiders grew ever lonelier and more cut off, and missed the carefree days when life on the island was easygoing and friendly. Now they noted that there were quarrels and tensions, arguments and physical confrontations. Some of the elders approached Harry Langendorf: "We did not formerly fight among ourselves like this, Harry Langendorf," they said. "We were placid and friendly birds, a bit shy perhaps, but warm and affectionate. Now the young are rude to the old, impatient with one another and critical of their parents. And the parents are fighting among themselves."

"Of course," said Harry Langendorf, "We must pay a price for progress, but we must be willing to pay it. Perfection comes only with striving, and striving, of necessity, will bring some hostility—especially at first. There must be some drive to sustain the pelican who seeks to soar far above the ordinary. Competition gives him energy. There will be time enough for leisure when we are perfect. Long enough have we been placid and friendly, and stupid and unproductive as well. Now we are gradually becoming the most admired of birds. The gulls pay us new respect, the cormorants are awed, even the sea lions know that there has been a transformation."

"But are we as happy as we were? Before we always had time, time to laugh and talk, time to rest and watch, time to love. What is the meaning of all this activity?"

"Activity is life," said Harry Langendorf, "Not to accomplish is to die. Long enough have we been satisfied with our traditions. Now we must form new ones. We will organize and restrict our fishing to brief periods. Only the old and helpless will be sitting on pier posts and staring out at the water. The important birds will be reaching for new records and flying to new skies."

"We will climb higher and higher. Even now there is evidence that there are fresh seas above this one and new horizons. We may be called upon to unite all the pelican species of the world. We do not know what our destiny is, but unless we strive with endless energy and boundless strength, we will decay and die. Mediocrity is the way of cowards, perfection is the only path for heroes."

"But is there nothing to be said for kindness and compassion, for leisure and enjoyment? Is not food a gift we should enjoy, are not the seas made to be seen and shared, are not the beauties of earth as wondrous as those of the skies?"

"Any mediocre fool can wander about the coast and the shallow waters. Only the perfect can reach beyond the heavens and earth."

Harry Langendorf was good with words. The old pelicans turned their heads away, lowered their bills, and waddled back to the rocks to talk with their friends. "It is a new day," they said. "Perhaps we have been wrong. Perhaps we have wasted our lives."

On occasions, Harry Langendorf flew off by himself, high above the other pelicans, far out to sea, up and down the coast, practicing higher dives, faster somersaults, quicker takeoffs. But most of all he flew higher and higher, far beyond the clouds, into the cold and rarefied reaches where pelicans had never gone. His head grew dizzy, his heart beat mightily, he heard new sounds and strange voices, and the young thrilled to the narration of his new adventures. He lead an expedition farther south than a pelican had ever traveled, another farther north than anyone dreamed possible. He traveled inland, not poking along in a leisurely way, not pausing to study the sights, but setting new records to spur the pelicans on to higher goals and more ambitious pursuits.

But much of the time, he was resolving new problems that arose. Several pelicans had been severely injured hitting the water at high speeds. He spent days at the shore showing them how to set and release their wings, how to break their falls with

their chests, how to enter the water without banging their heads; several others were not eating properly, so he arranged group feeding ventures; many were growing tense and nervous, so he devised recreational programs to relax them. Guards were set up to keep the gulls away, scouts were found to spot the best fishing areas on given days. There was no price that would not be paid in the striving for perfection.

The parents continued to complain that the young were insolent and angry. Quarrels were breaking out frequently on the island. Harry Langendorf's leadership was questioned, not only by the outsiders but by the elitists themselves. Even his son, Edward Langendorf, confronted him: "Sometimes you are a tyrant," he said. "Maybe it was better before."

"Do not ever say that," said Harry Langendorf. "You, of all pelicans. You are a Langendorf!"

Samantha Butterfield also seemed irritable and short-tempered. "You are always creating problems, Harry Langendorf," she said.

"It is not easy to seek perfection," he answered. "We will reach the stars, no matter what."

But at other times, when he was weary, Samantha Butterfield was there to prod him and push him on. "I am so proud of you," she said. "You can do so much, you are the pelican I dreamed of and never believed I would find." Thus he worked even harder, pushed his own children and the other young, marveling at their new record flights of height and distance, and dreamed of a colony of incredible strength and efficiency.

His own son, Edward, was the most accomplished of the young. For several months he was no match for Harry Langendorf, but he continued to compete. "You are a great flier, Edward Langendorf," said his friends, "But you are still not a match for your father."

"Give me time," he said.

The competition between them grew more vigorous. When Edward flew high, Harry Langendorf flew higher. When Edward dove with blinding speed, Harry Langendorf dove faster. When Edward speared a large fish, Harry Langendorf speared a bigger one. The whole colony talked about their competition. And in the rare times the family was together, they talked tirelessly of their accomplishments. They were beautiful together, healthy and lean, alert and active, proud and determined to attain perfection.

"What is perfection?" asked his daughter.

"You will know when you reach it," he said. "It is the outer limits of pelican fulfillment."

"But are there any limits?" asked Edward.

"I have wondered many times, but I am not sure. Continue to strive, continue to reach; seek to be perfect," said Harry Langendorf.

"We will," said Mary Langendorf.

He nodded to her. She was lean and intense, proud and

strong like her mother. She had not the talent of Edward, but she was determined and ambitious and fiercely competitive.

"Perhaps we should take a trip together," said Harry Langendorf. "It would be good to be with our own family for a change."

Samantha and the children agreed. They set out to the north and flew together along the California coast. No family had ever flown as fast, no parents had ever been as proud. They rested in one of the little bays, fished to recapture their strength, and headed out to the ocean.

"I am going to fly high," said Edward.

"Let's all do it," said Mary.

Samantha and Harry Langendorf followed them with excitement. Higher and higher they went. Above the clouds into the thin and cold air. "I am going to dive," said Edward.

"Not from here," said Harry Langendorf. "It is too high, you are not yet ready to dive from here. I could not do it myself."

"I will do it then," said Edward. "I want to be perfect."

"You are not yet capable," said Harry Langendorf.

"You are only afraid I will surpass you," said Edward.

"Do not be insolent," said Harry Langendorf. "I know what you are capable of."

"No one knows that," said Edward.

Before Harry Langendorf could say another word, Edward pulled his wings tight against his body and plunged towards the sea.

"He'll kill himself," said Harry Langendorf. He raced after him, diving and checking his speed. Even so, he had all he could do to hang on. He shot through the clouds into the clear skies and, far below, heard the echoing smack of Edward's body hit the water. In a few seconds he was in the water next to his son. But he knew it was too late.

Samantha Butterfield and Mary Langendorf approached.

"He is dead," said Harry Langendorf. "Our son is dead. What have we done!" He beat his wings against the water, paused and pecked disconsolately at the bill of his son. His pouch will never open again," said Harry Langendorf.

Samantha was obviously moved but she seemed to recover quickly. "He died trying to be a perfect pelican. What more noble death could there be? We should be very proud."

"But he is dead," said Harry Langendorf.

"He did what he wanted, Harry Langendorf," said Mary. "He continued to strive until the end. I am very proud of my brother."

"My son is dead," groaned Harry Langendorf. "I killed my son."

"No," said Samantha Butterfield, "He chose his own way. There will be other children, other perfect children who will reach the stars. Come, Harry Langendorf, we must go."

"But we cannot leave him here. The birds and fish will rip the flesh from his bones," said Harry Langendorf. "I will not leave him here."

"Then you must take care of him," said Samantha Butterfield. "Come, Mary Langendorf, we will return to the island to celebrate the memory of this noble son. We shall see you when you return, Harry Langendorf."

But he did not hear her. The tears were streaming down his face. Already the body of his son was heavy with water. He could not lift him from the waves. He tried fiercely to pull him up, then to waddle across the water and to take flight. But it was impossible. So he began to drag him through the waves weeping and groaning, bleeding from the mouth. As evening approached, the waves grew higher and tossed him about. Suddenly a giant wave tore the body of Edward Langendorf from his bill and he saw the body of his dead son one last time on the crest of a giant wave before it was buried in the sea.

Harry Langendorf Pelican was exhausted. Only with the greatest effort could he make his way to the land. He crawled up on the shore, found a place among the rocks high above the water and fell into a deep sleep. When he awoke the sun was already high in the heavens. His whole body ached, dried blood covered his bill. He rose up weakly, washed himself in the shallow water, caught a few fish and began the long flight back to the island.

"I cannot go back," he thought, "not now." His whole body was heavy with the sadness of his heart and the great physical strain of the previous evening. He made his way slowly towards the reef of the dead, the sacred spot where he had mourned his mother's disappearance. He had not been there for some time.

When he arrived, he heard the feeble breathing of the dying who stared vacantly out to sea, saw them lose control of their heads like newborn babies, watched them weary and unable to fly. He saw as well the bones of the dead, bleached white in the sun, worn smooth by the water, tossed carelessly about by the scavengers and the wind.

"O Edward, Edward, my son!" he cried. "I never knew you my son, I never knew you."

A strange feeling came upon him and he began to cry helplessly. It was more than grief over Edward's death. Suddenly he felt powerless. He did not want to fly high above the clouds, he did not want to dive at blinding speeds, he wanted only to rest and ponder. Wild thoughts came into his head, strange visions crowded his imagination, whispered voices invaded his consciousness. He sat still for many hours, unable to move. The fog came and settled over the reef, the sun disappeared and he pulled his neck into his shoulders, lowered his bill, and sobbed quite helplessly.

He chided himself: "I've got to pull myself together. I am the most respected pelican who ever lived. I can fly higher than anyone, dive with greater speed, cover greater distances. I have no limits. I can be perfect. I must be perfect."

But his sobs continued as the night grew colder and the fog thicker. He barely slept. It was difficult to know when he was sleeping and when he was awake. He had visions of thousands of pelicans chasing him through the sky, storming after him, struggling to reach him, fighting to overtake him. He could not control his weird and wild thoughts, he could not stop his sobbing.

He thought of Samantha Butterfield. He knew what she expected of him, how proud she was, how relentless in her ambition. He thought of Edward with acute pain, he thought of Mary. He had never really known his family, not even Samantha. She was strength to him, ambition and power, but he had never really known her. There had been no time to know anyone, no time for gentle and quiet picnics on the beach, no time to explore the rocks along the coast, no time to play games with the sea lions or to give exciting rides to the Heerman's gulls who love to sit astride the pelicans.

He tried to control himself, to stop his trembling. He felt foolish and frightened, helpless and alone. "I have no friends, only admirers. I have no joy, only ambition and endless striving. There is no goal which will satisfy me, no accomplishment which seems to give me rest. I do not know what to do."

He remained on the reef for many weeks, eating only what was necessary, feeling the waves lapping at his feathers, listening to the wind and watching the ancient pelicans die. His whole body seemed loose and helpless. "Maybe I am going to die," he said, and he trembled all the more. "Maybe this is what death is."

But death did not come, only feelings of utter loneliness, and fear, and endless questions. The strength he once felt seemed to be disappearing. It was not that he could not fly as once he had; it seemed that he had lost the desire. Something had happened and he did not know what it was.

At first he felt it was guilt over Edward's death, but as the weeks wore on, the guilt seemed to disappear. "I have accepted Edward's death," he said aloud. "I accept my responsibility, I did the best I knew how. I only wish it could have been otherwise, but I have done my grieving. Soon I must return to the island. There is Samantha to think of, and Mary, and the others."

He spent a few final days on the reef of the dead, studying the waves and absorbing the energy of the sun. He felt the silence of the sunset touch him deep within his heart and the excitement of the sunrise filled his whole body with a quiet peace. Then, one cloudless day, he made his way back to the colony.

When he reached the island he became suddenly aware of the intensity and frenzy there in contrast to the silence of the reef. The frenetic energy which once had pleased him now troubled him.

"Where have you been, Harry Langendorf? We missed you!" called the young. "We have made new records."

"Have you been happy?" he asked.

"Very happy," they said, "We are going to be perfect pelicans."

Samantha Butterfield seemed angry with him: "Where have you been Harry Langendorf? Life goes on, there are a million things to do."

"There is time," he said slowly. "There is time."

"But there is not time," said Samantha, "Mary needs your direction, and there have been many quarrels among Edward's friends. The young need more training, and the elders are questioning your leadership. Come fly high and dive swiftly, Harry Langendorf, more swiftly than ever before. Show everyone that you have returned."

Harry Langendorf did not move. He looked over the island, then slowly waddled down to walk among the old and infirm, to chat with them and laugh about trips made long before. They talked of the sardines that once were as thick as rain, they told of the great tropical squalls they had endured, they recalled the year of the heavy fog. He sat with them for a long time, listened quietly, and watched the sun go down in silence.

"We are sorry about your son," said an old pelican.

"I am sorry, too," said Harry Langendorf, "Very sorry. I miss him very much. We could have been good friends."

"You seem different, Harry Langendorf," said one of the others, "Softer and wiser somehow."

"I am different," said Harry Langendorf.

The young approached him. "Fly with us to the north, Harry Langendorf, we want to break the speed and distance record. We need you."

"Not now," he said. "I seem to be very tired."

They were astonished. Harry Langendorf had never admitted weariness. He had always seemed indomitable, eternally powerful. "You will live forever, Harry Langendorf," they said.

"No, someday I too will die," he said quietly.

"But you will be the perfect pelican, Harry Langendorf. Someday we will all be perfect."

"It does not seem important," he said.

The colony was tense with curiosity and excitement. Small groups gathered to talk in quiet tones. "What has happened to him?" they asked. "He seems to have lost his energy and vision."

The elders approached him: "We are all sorry about your son, Harry Langendorf, but you cannot grieve forever. We need you."

"I am not grieving anymore," he said.

"It is your guilt," said one of the sages. "Guilt takes away energy."

"Indeed it does," said Harry Langendorf. "But I do not feel guilty. I have accepted Edward's death. I only regret that I did not get to know him well. But that is over now. I am no longer sad," he said. "I feel quite peaceful, almost joyous."

"Then soon you will lead us again?" they asked. "There has

been much confusion without you; there has been wrangling and quarreling, disputes and bitter confrontations."

"I will not be the leader I was," he said. "I am different now. I do not know why, but I am different."

"It is not easy to lose your firstborn son," they said.

"I know that," said Harry Langendorf. "But I really had no son, nor did he have a father."

"Then what do you propose to do?" they asked.

"I have no proposals," he said with a smile. "I want to know my friends, to enjoy them. And I want to enjoy myself."

"But you have accomplished so much, Harry Langendorf. You have had so much to enjoy. We have been very proud of you."

"But you do not know me," said Harry Langendorf.

They walked away confused.

Samantha was outraged and approached him privately: "What in the world is wrong with you? You go away for a few weeks and you return like a mumbling fool. You have lost your poise and power, you have abandoned your dignity. I will not put up with it. Even your daughter, who admired you so, is embarrassed to tears. She thinks you had love only for Edward."

"I will tell her otherwise," said Harry Langendorf. "I have never loved her more. Nor you either."

"Who needs your weak, listless, love?" she said. "I married Harry Langendorf, the intense and dynamic pelican. I will not accept this lollygagging substitute. You either act like you once did or forget about me and Mary."

"Samantha—" he said.

"Don't Samantha me," she answered. "You are not the pelican I knew. You have become dull and boring!"

"I do not feel dull and boring," he said. "I think I am beginning to feel good for the first time in my adult life."

"Then you are not going to be like you were?" she asked.

"Not like I was," said Harry Langendorf.

"Then forget about your family," said Samantha Butterfield. "I should have known you couldn't rise above your peasant stock." She waddled briskly away.

It was strange to be alone. Somehow Samantha Butterfield had always been his. He had never really known her, but she was always there and the sound of her voice and the flutter of her wings were home to him. He liked her odor, the color of her pouch, the long brown feathers at the back of her neck. There had been happy days. He thought of their courtship, of handing her twigs and sea grass to soften the nest. He thought of the long nights when she had warmed the eggs and the hours he had relieved her with joy and expectation. Now he was alone.

He wandered down to the edge of the rocks. Edward's friends approached him. They looked strong and sure of themselves: "We have mastered the left bank turn at incredible speed," they said. "We have flown higher than ever before,

Harry Langendorf. We shall fly higher than you."

"I am sure you will," said Harry Langendorf. "But for what reason?"

"You taught us to fly higher and higher," they said. "You taught us to strive and to seek perfection!"

"I taught you only what I thought was right," said Harry Langendorf. "I taught you what I myself had learned from others. Now I think differently about my life."

"But what has changed you, Harry Langendorf?" they asked.

"I do not know what has changed me," he said.

There was silence. They could not believe his words. Harry Langendorf had always been so sure, now he sounded hesitant and uncertain. He even looked different. His face was softer, his eyes more gentle, his head was not as erect and his wings moved more slowly and quietly when he talked.

They moved away. "He has no strength," they said. "He has lost his courage!" They stood together staring out at the sea. Suddenly one of them shouted: "Warren Covington can be our leader. He has set all of the records since Edward's death. No one is stronger and more powerful than Warren Covington."

Warren Covington was taken aback. He enjoyed the position that his power had given him among his fellows and he took great pride in the honors that were heaped on him, but he had not considered himself ready to be the established leader. "I am not sure," he said.

"You must be," they said. "You are the obvious leader."

Warren Covington hesitated. He had competed openly with Edward before his tragic death and had secretly resented the talent and power of Harry Langendorf, but he had never imagined that he might replace him. Harry Langendorf was almost an institution, and it took several minutes for Warren Covington to quiet his racing mind. He saw the elders bow respectfully to him, watched, in fantasy, the sages consult him seriously and ponder his decisions. A new feeling began to take possession of him and the first taste of power was sweet and almost intoxicating. He could be their leader. He could be more than a talented pelican, he could lead them to the stars.

He awoke as if from a dream: "I will be your leader," said Warren Covington quietly. The very tone of his voice was stronger and more resonant. "We will reach the moon. We will live forever."

"We will follow you, Warren Covington!" they said. "We will try to surpass you. There are no limits, we will live forever."

They walked back to Harry Langendorf. "We do not need you!" they said, "Warren Covington will lead us to the stars."

"Yes I shall!" said Warren Covington.

Harry Langendorf said nothing. He waddled over to some rocks on the far side of the island. A few young pelicans were gathered there, laughing and playing games. "You are Harry Langendorf!" they said with awe.

"Yes I am," he said.

"We have never really met you," they said. "We were always too slow and awkward to be perfect pelicans."

"It is not important to be perfect pelicans," he said. "You seem to be happy pelicans."

"But we cannot fly beyond the clouds," they said.

"You can fly," said Harry Langendorf, "and that is joy enough. To strive is never to be satisfied. You can catch enough fish to eat, you can soar and scale and feel the breeze. You can see the sun."

"But we are not respected," they said. "We are only tolerated."

"It is only important that you respect yourselves," said Harry Langendorf.

"But we will never reach the stars, Harry Langendorf."

"The stars are more beautiful from here," he said. "Besides, you yourselves are as beautiful as the stars."

"But we are dull and boring," they said.

"You do not seem dull and boring to me," said Harry Langendorf. "You seem happy and beautiful. Come we will take a little trip."

"But we cannot fly with you," they said. "We are no match for you. You will put us to shame and the entire colony will laugh at us."

"Come," he said, "We will fly simply to enjoy ourselves."

He led them from the island, across the water towards the

coastline, floating along gracefully over the tips of the waves. Occasionally they dove for fish, laughed when they hit their heads on the water, laughed when they clumsily attempted to take off. "Our takeoffs are not very fast, Harry Langendorf," they said. "But they are fun," he answered. "You are beautiful birds, shaped and formed through hundreds of centuries, friends of the sea and brothers of the very fish you eat."

They flew into a little fishing village, paused for an hour or so to watch the fishermen unload their catch on the pier, kingfish and corvina, mackerel and halibut, sea turtles and giant totuava. They laughed at the beady-eyed lobsters and listened attentively when Harry Langendorf told them how the lobsters lived in quiet caves and found their way about with long antennae. Then he led them along the beach to watch the men and boys dig for Pismo clams with pitchforks, then across the rocks where the sea lions were sliding down into the waves. They flew inland and watched the women grind corn to make tortillas, saw them making pottery from damp clay and marveled at the motion of their hands.

"Hands are funny," said one of the young birds. "They look like anchovies flopping on the sand." Harry Langendorf and all the other pelicans laughed uproariously. "We have never had such a good time, Harry Langendorf," they said. "Neither have I," said Harry Langendorf. They flew a few miles north along the coastline, watched a school of porpoise dancing through the water, flew high to catch the thermal drafts, and floated over the mountain tops.

"Let's catch some fish," said Harry Langendorf. They followed him over the waves until he spotted the water churning and knew the fish were on the surface. He dove and they followed. "These are fresh and healthy fish," he said, and they all ate hungrily. "We are not as graceful or as quick as you, Harry Langendorf," they said.

"The fish don't seem to notice," said Harry Langendorf. They all laughed loudly and continued to fill their pouches. When they had eaten their fill, they followed Harry Langendorf back to the island, their wings moving swiftly across the sky, their eyes excited and alive. "We have had such a good time, Harry Langendorf," they called.

"Indeed we have," said Harry Langendorf.

There was great anger and resentment on the island when they returned. Warren Covington and his friends were hostile and critical. So were many of the elders. Samantha Butterfield was livid. "Look at him!" she said. "Wandering around aimlessly, unconcerned, not caring about growth and perfection. There is so little time and so much to be accomplished!"

Harry Langendorf and his new friends wandered down to the edge of the rocks and began chatting with the old pelicans who sat there staring out at the sea. "We had so much fun," the young pelicans said. "Harry Langendorf showed us everything, and tomorrow we will go out again."

"Maybe we'll take a trip up the coast before the mating season begins," said Harry Langendorf.

"Will we go hundreds of miles?" they asked.

"It does not matter how far we go," he said.

The elders stood at the outside of the circle and motioned to Harry Langendorf to join them in a conference. He waddled towards them with a warm smile. "We had a nice day," he said.

"You have lost your vision," they said angrily.

"No, I think I have found it," said Harry Langendorf. "I have never felt better in my life."

"Life is not for feeling better," they said. "Life is for striving and accomplishment, for discipline and progress and growth, new achievements and bold advances. Then you will deserve to feel better."

Harry Langendorf laughed: "What's wrong with watching the fishermen and enjoying the sea lions? There is so much to see, so much to enjoy. And what's wrong with just sitting and staring out to sea? I am learning to do nothing," he said with a smile.

"You are dragging us down," they said. "The young will lose their energy and ambition. There is so little time to improve ourselves. We can be great birds flying high above the heavens, moving beyond the earth into unknown atmosphere and unheard of horizons."

"Or we can watch the sunset," said Harry Langendorf turning away.

"But you are missing so many opportunities to improve yourself. Such opportunities never come again."

"Opportunities return," said Harry Langendorf quietly.

"You have grown aimless and undisciplined, Harry Langendorf," they said.

"I hope so," he said. "It has not been easy."

"But is it wrong to aspire to fly higher and higher and faster and faster?" they asked.

"Not if you want to," he said. "But I don't really want to. It was expected of me and I expected it of others."

"You fear competition," said one of the elders. "You realize that the young will surpass you and you are afraid."

"Sometimes I am afraid," said Harry Langendorf. "But I am not afraid of being surpassed. Competition has not made me happy."

"What if everyone were like you?" they asked. "Who would take responsibility?"

"I do not know," said Harry Langendorf, "but I can be responsible without competing."

"You are indeed mad," they said.

"Perhaps I am. But we have talked enough. Now I would like to watch the final moments of the sunset." He turned away.

The water was quiet now, the waves lapping gently at the rocks. The pelicans gathered in silence on the shore. A single ship was framed against the declining sun and seemed to be

on fire. A giant path of water from sun to shore shone with an iridescent gold. There was nothing to say, it was too beautiful.

The following day Harry Langendorf awakened early. The sun was beginning to rise and the air was damp and cold. He shivered and smiled gently. It would be a clear day, great for rambling along the coast and taking a trip north. The young birds had never seen a large city with its cars and buildings, its parks and quiet bays. He would fly with them over grassy hills and serene lakes, across farmlands and sand dunes. They would see new and unfamiliar birds and float above surfers and tankers and sailing ships.

Gradually the sun began to warm the air and the pelicans were starting to waddle about the island. Some flew out to find fish, others simply stared at the sea or watched the little crabs crawl over the rocks and dodge the waves. Warren Covington and his numerous followers were planning a new conquest. "We will let them know that there is more to life than waddling about the rocks and cramming their pouches with fish."

The novices were excited. "We will break all the old flying records," they said. "We will dive from a thousand feet."

Warren laughed. "A thousand feet is nothing. We will dive from ten thousand feet and pull out just above the water. Never set yourself such meager goals or you will end up sitting on the poles of decaying piers watching gulls and fishermen, like Harry Langendorf."

They all laughed and set out on their exciting new challenge.

On the other side of the island, Harry Langendorf was preparing his expedition. "It is still several weeks until the mating season," he said, "so we can take a trip to the north. We should all eat well before we leave because we may have some trouble, at first, finding fresh fish. The fish in the north are not as healthy as those around here."

One of the older birds approached him: "I would like to go with you, Harry Langendorf. So would some of my friends, but we don't fly as fast as you, not even as fast as the young birds."

"It does not matter," said Harry Langendorf, "There is no hurry. Come with us, you will add to the pleasure of our trip. We will take our time; there is so much to see, so much to enjoy."

The old pelicans were delighted. New life stirred in their wings. "We won't set any records," they said with a laugh. "Don't count on me to catch your fish," said Harry with a smile. "So get those wings in shape."

They set out across the water, old and young, flying in an awkward formation. "The gulls will think we've gone mad," said the old pelicans with delight. "We'll tell them it's a funeral procession," said Harry Langendorf. They reached the mainland, fished for breakfast, rested for awhile, and then began to fly north along the coast. "How far will we go?" they asked. "Who knows?" said Harry Langendorf.

It was a great day. They saw a huge manta ray floating along under the surface of the water like a velvet blanket. They saw him rise up above the water and flap mightily to shake off the barnacles, and farther out, they saw a small group of grey whales spouting and hissing their way north to the Bering Sea with two newborn babies. They saw porpoises and sailing ships, tankers and fishing boats, precipitous cliffs and little fishing villages along the shore. They rested amid the ruins of an old mission, explored strange rocks and piles of kelp, sat with the sandpipers and gulls. "We have never had such fun, Harry Langendorf," they said. "We have never seen such sights."

They camped for the night, dove for fish in quiet lagoons, laughed at one another, told stories of strange occurrences in the past. The old were teeming with stories to tell, of the phantom pelican who returned every year to the top of a volcano where the gulls had killed his children, and of the year the volcano erupted and killed thousands of gulls in angry vengeance. After that the phantom, somehow appeased, never returned again. Harry Langendorf told of the reef where he had watched the ancient pelicans die, of ghostly sounds that resounded in the thick fog, of the strange disappearance of his beloved mother. And they talked of funny things as well, of the comical Wally Pelican who could never get up enough speed to fly. They laughed till they were almost sick when one of the old birds mimicked Wally's frantic efforts to take off. He would paddle his feet across the water and flap his wings wildly until he fell exhausted on the waves. They told of the weird Duncan Pelican who used to knock himself cold every time he dove. "He couldn't get his pouch open and just fell on his head." And Fats Pelican who used to fill his pouch so full that he almost drowned.

They flew over a giant city, saw tall buildings and towering trees, green grass and giant smokestacks like the steaming geysers in the mountains. They saw streams of cars and trucks, crowded streets and schoolchildren. They saw a zoo with birds and animals in cages, cats and dogs prowling the streets, modern fishing boats and giant sailing ships crowded into harbors. "We will never forget this trip, Harry Langendorf, we have seen a whole new world."

"We have seen each other," said Harry Langendorf. They sat for hours looking out to sea, sat on sandbars until the rising waters lapped at their feet; they fished when they needed to, watched the sun set each evening, and woke early to see it rise. "The sun is the most beautiful gift of all," they said.

And then it was time to return. They started the flight south, moving leisurely, without plans, stopping often to rest, pausing to enjoy the sea and its wonders, and taking time to examine what interested them; they camped early in the evening to talk and watch the sunset in silence. "We have not set any records," they said. "Maybe there are no records to set," said Harry Langendorf.

When they returned to the island, the very old and the weak were anxious to hear the story of their travels. They talked excitedly, told and retold their tales, and gathered together to watch the sun and the sea. The elders approached Harry Langendorf. "We would like to have a discussion with you," they said. "It can wait until tomorrow," said Harry Langendorf, "I do not feel like talking now. I want to watch the sun in silence."

In the morning the elders approached him again. "I want to have my breakfast first," said Harry Langendorf, "and enjoy for a few minutes the warmth of the morning sun." They waited impatiently; the whole colony was aware of the approaching encounter.

An hour or so later, Harry Langendorf joined them at a private corner of the island. They did not hesitate to get down to business immediately: "We are exceedingly disappointed in you," they said. "You have abandoned your responsibility to the young—even to your wife and family."

"My wife is quite able to take care of herself—and me—and you—and several others if need be," he said with a smile.

"You have become aimless," they said. "You have lost your drive and direction. The young cannot look up to you. What are you trying to accomplish, Harry Langendorf?"

"I am not trying to accomplish anything," said Harry Langendorf, "I am living my life."

"You have abandoned leadership of the colony," they said.

"I am not a leader," he said. "I have no disciples, I have only friends."

"But who will teach the young wisdom and discipline?"

"Wisdom is not taught," said Harry Langendorf. "Systems are taught. Wisdom comes from experiencing life, or it never comes at all. And life is its own discipline."

"You would then leave all pelicans at their present level of development, Harry Langendorf, by encouraging them to be idle and satisfied, by ignoring our programs and systems?"

"The young pelicans do not seem interested in systems until they are obliged to be. They seem content to fly and eat, to love and learn, to play and enjoy. So am I."

"And you would shirk your responsibilities?"

"I do not think so. Those things I once felt obligated to do, now seem simply a part of my life. They became 'responsibilities' when I drove myself to excel."

"But what produces growth and progress, Harry Langendorf?"

"Perhaps if we are not pushed and prodded or made to feel ashamed, we will achieve our growth—and our joy as well."

"But you must seek to find, Harry Langendorf!" they said.

"No," he said; "it seems to be in not seeking that I find."

"Is it to do nothing, then, to accomplish nothing?"

"No," said Harry Langendorf. "It is to do more and to have more energy than I ever had in striving. It is to be one with life."

"Where is this life, Harry Langendorf?"

"It is within," he said.

"And how does one discover it?" they asked.

"Perhaps by not looking for it, by not seeking, by permitting one's self to be. Perhaps it is not for everyone."

"Who told you all of this, Harry Langendorf?"

"It is not something that can be told," he said. "I learned it from suffering and joy, love and friendship—from living."

"You are a revolutionary, an anarchist and rebel!" they said angrily.

Harry Langendorf smiled. "No," he said, "I am just a happy pelican who is beginning to live."

"Is there no place for faith, Harry Langendorf?"

"Yes, perhaps—faith in one's own beauty and that of others."

"And what is your goal?" they asked.

"I do not seem to need a goal," he said. "Living seems to be all—and dying."

"What lies after death?" they asked.

"I do not know," said Harry Langendorf. "Perhaps something beautiful, perhaps nothing. It does not seem important."

"You are very selfish, Harry Langendorf. You would not help others in time of need."

"I think I will help others," said Harry Langendorf, "But I do not think of myself as a helper."

"You live with illusions, Harry Langendorf," they said.

"Perhaps," he said. "But at present, for me, time is the illusion—and striving. Titles are an illusion—and progress."

"But you want us to change, Harry Langendorf, and to be like you."

"No," he said. "I can only tell you who I am. You must decide who you are."

"But if everyone did as they pleased, Harry Langendorf, we would destroy ourselves," they said.

"I think we destroy ourselves when we do not do what pleases us," he said.

"Life is harder than you make it, Harry Langendorf."

"Maybe we make it hard by trying to live up to what others expect of us."

"You are weird and strange, Harry Langendorf. Perhaps you are very sick."

"I feel very good," said Harry Langendorf. "But I have talked too much. After a point, words seem futile."

"Will you never fly above the clouds again, Harry Langendorf?" one of them asked wistfully. "You were beautiful to see."

Harry Langendorf laughed: "Sometimes I will when it gives me joy. I do many things I always did but I feel differently when I do them."

"It is easy to be lazy, Harry Langendorf," they said.

"Not for me," said Harry Langendorf. "I'm just learning."

It was mating season and the male pelicans began building their nests, and Harry Langendorf took great pleasure in the construction. Some of the young insisted on helping him. He did not work as fiercely as before, but he enjoyed searching for twigs and soft strands of grass, and wove them lovingly and carefully into the giant nest. He had selected a new site since he could not bring himself to reconstruct the nest he once shared with Samantha. When his nest was completed, he attended it carefully waiting for the approach of the females.

But no one came. After several days of waiting, he realized no one was going to come so he stopped watching. He watched the others close by falling in love, working together, taking their practice flights to learn the routes of easy access to the nest in case of danger. He felt very lonely.

"I will have to learn to live alone," he said. He saw Samantha with her new mate and realized that she looked more beautiful than ever. He wandered down to the edge of the rocks, nodded to some of his young friends who were fishing close to shore, and began chatting with some of the older pelicans he had grown to love.

"You seem sad, Harry Langendorf," they said.

"I guess I am a little sad," he said, "But the ocean and the sun will make me feel better." He flew out to sea a mile or so, flew thousands of feet up to catch the thermal drafts and floated in the warm sun across the mountains. Later he scaled over the waters, ate a few fish, and returned late in the afternoon to the island to watch the declining sun.

Soon enough the other pelicans' eggs were hatched, and he enjoyed bringing a huge pouchful of food back to the squawking young. He fished vigorously, dropped off a few snacks for the sick and the old, swapped stories with them about special experiences, and laughed far into the night. Harry Langendorf was happy again.

Sometimes, a few of the young birds would gather around him to listen to the stories he shared, or even follow him to the mainland to see the sights, or sit quietly with him in one of his favorite spots to watch the setting sun. He showed them the sea lions at play, spotted the line of porpoises skipping through the waters, took them to a quiet lagoon where they saw monstrous grey whales attending their young.

All the while the elders said nothing. They knew that Harry Langendorf had lost his influence on the island and they felt the slight given him by the females of the colony was reprimand enough.

Gradually his circle of young friends began to grow. But usually it was not the most talented who came to him. The powerful flyers preferred the company of Warren Covington and the island rang with their enthusiasm for the new records they set.

"You can fly higher than any pelican in the world, Warren

Covington," said his admirers.

"It is true," said Warren Covington, "But we must never rest. We must strive until we pass on to higher skies and cleaner waters."

"Teach us all you know, Warren Covington. Take us from the scavenging pelicans who loll about the beaches and the piers. Take us from the lazy pelicans who follow Harry Langendorf about, sightseeing and listening to his stories."

"You must have courage and great faith," said Warren Covington. "You must believe that you can accomplish everything."

"We do believe," they said. "We will fly forever—in this world and the next."

Harry Langendorf continued his little trips up and down the coast. On especially nice days, several of the older birds flew along. "It is so much fun to be with you, Harry Langendorf," they said.

"And I enjoy you," said Harry Langendorf.

"You do not push us or prod us," said the young. "Should not our life be difficult?"

"Only if you want it so," said Harry Langendorf.

The days passed quickly, summer blending into fall and passing into winter. One day in the spring there was great excitement on the island. Warren Covington had broken the

free-fall record of Harry Langendorf, and now was the proud-
est pelican of all time. In the evening, all the pelicans of the
colony gathered to honor him. The elders placed a garland of
sea grass around his neck, and the assembled group lifted their
bills to the sky and stretched their pouches open wide in joy
and celebration. Harry Langendorf, at the edge of the crowd,
lifted his bill as well.

"Are you not troubled, Harry Langendorf?" said some of
his friends. "Are you not a little jealous—and hurt—because
you are left out?"

"Maybe a little," said Harry Langendorf, "But I am glad that
Warren Covington seems happy."

"But you should be honored as well," they said.

"I do not want to be honored," he said.

Another mating season passed, and yet another, and now
the time was upon them again. Harry Langendorf built his nest
as before and, again, for several days no one came. He began
to stare out at the sea, to fly along the shore, to watch the
merriment and excitement of the nuptials everywhere. One
afternoon, while he was sitting on the nest not really expecting
any company since all the women were taken, a frail-looking
bird approached him, bowed a few times weakly, lifted her
bill and joined him in the nest. She was not too much to look
at, somewhat skinny and unkempt, feathers a bit disheveled,

pouch spotted with weak colors. But her eyes were soft and incredibly beautiful, like his mother's.

He stared at her for several moments, then bowed to her in love, pecked at her bill affectionately, and handed her a few strands of grass to soften the nest. "You are beautiful," she said. And indeed he was, with the bright gold patch of full manhood resplendent on his head and chest. "You are beautiful as well," he said. "Who are you? I have never seen you before."

"I am Dolores Larson," she said. "My people are from much farther north. I lost my way and landed here. But I know I am not beautiful."

"I think you are beautiful," said Harry Langendorf, "But perhaps you would not want me." He told her the story of his life on the island, from the death of his mother to the rejection by the elders.

"It does not matter," she said. "I love you, but I cannot give you much. I tire very easily and my feathers have lost their sheen."

"You have given me much already," he said. "You are soft and warm, and the gentleness in your eyes touches me beyond all words." And later in the day he mated with her in joy.

When she laid the eggs, it was obvious that they were not healthy. The shells were soft and she was deeply disappointed.

"Do not feel bad," said Harry Langendorf, "There will be another year. Many of our females have laid soft eggs. It is from the polluted fish in the sea. We will travel farther south and east to the Sea of Cortez and find fresher fish to nourish you back to health. Next year you will have fat and squawking babies. Now fly down to the shore and I will get rid of the eggs." She obeyed and with his eyes moist, Harry Langendorf pushed the eggs out of the nest into the cactus.

Their days together were happy ones. He guided Dolores Larson to the choice fish and shared with her the special sights that delighted his heart. Side by side they watched the sun go down every night and woke up early every morning, wherever they were, to watch it rise. "The sun is our friend," said Dolores Larson. "Indeed it is," said Harry Langendorf.

After a year of travel and rest, a year of being together with their friends, it was mating time again. Dolores Larson at last had the children they desired. A boy and girl, too beautiful for words. They were average children, ate reasonably well, learned to fish and fly like all the others, and loved the trips up and down the shoreline with Harry Langendorf and Dolores Larson and all their friends.

Dolores was never accepted by the elite of the island. They laughed at her waddling gait, secretly made fun of Harry Langendorf for mating with such an ugly pelican, and criticized his very average children. Sometimes Dolores would say to him: "I am not good enough for you Harry Langendorf. You deserve much better."

"I love you," he said with a smile, "to me you are more beautiful than any words."

When the children were able to take care of themselves, Harry Langendorf and Dolores Larson joined a small expedition of young pelicans, and a few of the older ones, to spend a few months far to the south. They delighted in the sights of the sea and land, celebrated the sun, slid cautiously through the fog, sensed storms and hid from them, cuddling in caves along the coast. Late in the fall they returned to their island and heard about the marvelous exploits of Warren Covington and his friends. There was no stopping them, they would eventually fly above the sky.

Harry Langendorf and Dolores Larson took their place on the shabbier side of the island with their friends. They learned of an old pelican who had died several weeks ago, learned that three of the infants had been murdered by the gulls, and heard stories about the strengths and weaknesses of the younger generation.

"There have been fierce quarrels on the islands, Harry Langendorf," they said. "Warren Covington has been challenged for the leadership. Mary Langendorf's husband, David McCarthy, has organized a large group of dissenters and there have been many deaths and serious injuries. One of Mary Langendorf's children was killed, not by the gulls, but by David's enemies."

Harry Langendorf looked as if he had been struck a heavy blow. "Oh, I must go to her!" he said. He rose up quickly and flew across the island. He saw Mary Langendorf surrounded by a large group of friends and party members.

"Mary Langendorf," he said. "I am so sorry about your child. I just returned from an expedition to the south. I am really very sorry."

"I don't need you," she said. "You were never here when we needed you. Now the whole island is in confusion. You could have led us to great heights, Harry Langendorf, but you were afraid. Go back with friends who expect nothing of you."

Harry Langendorf was very sad. There was nothing more he could say. He heard the arguments and threats ringing through the island. He saw the confusion and the fears. The young still talked of new feats and glorious accomplishments.

"David McCarthy will take us higher than Warren Covington ever dreamed," they said. "No one will stand in his way."

"Warren Covington still has all the records," said his friends. "No one will ever match him."

"It is only a matter of time," said the friends of David McCarthy. "Warren Covington will never lead us again."

The elders were divided. "We need a change," said some. "Warren Covington will not listen to anyone. The schools have been fierce and disorganized. There is quarreling and a lack of discipline. The young refuse to cooperate."

"It is the fault of the teachers," said others. "It is not the fault of Warren Covington. The followers of David McCarthy have undermined his efforts."

Harry Langendorf returned to the other side of the island. "There are many quarrels," he said.

"Perhaps you could do something, Harry Langendorf," said Dolores Larson. "You are good with words."

"There is nothing anyone can do," said Harry Langendorf. "No one listens to anyone else. There is too much anger and resentment. The situation is explosive, but it must run its course."

He settled down next to Dolores Larson and listened to the young tell of the wonders they saw in their travels. The old talked of former times, and the eyes of the young grew wide with excitement. Later in the evening Harry Langendorf spoke to the whole group: "I think we should move to an island farther south," he said, "The fish here are not healthy anymore, and there were too many thin eggs this year. Dolores and I are going to move and we invite as many of you as would like to come with us."

"But we should not leave when there is trouble on the island," said one of the old pelicans. "We cannot abandon our brothers when they are in trouble."

"I do not think there is anything we can do," said Harry Langendorf. "They do not want advice, nor are we their saviors. We can only be their friends and they do not want that."

"Can we invite some of them to go with us?" asked one of the young.

"Of course," said Harry Langendorf. "We are not running away from them. We just want to find better fish and healthier surroundings."

The next day they made plans to move. Most of Harry Langendorf's friends decided to move with him farther south. Some few decided to remain on the island, and a few others wanted to seek out other islands they had visited and particularly liked. The good-byes were warm and affectionate.

"We will not really say 'good-bye' to one another," said Harry Langendorf. "Because we will see each other in our travels."

A few of the pelicans from the other side of the island asked to go along and were welcomed graciously.

Harry Langendorf flew across the island to bid good-bye to Mary Langendorf and Samantha Butterfield. Mary nodded to him coldly and Samantha ignored him entirely.

The party set out across the water and made their way along the coastline to the south. They traveled almost three hundred miles until they found the island which was to be their new home.

"It is beautiful," they said. "There are fresh fish to eat, sea lions and birds to play with, and beautiful rocks on which to build our nests."

"We will love it here," said the old.

"The sunsets are incredible," said Harry Langendorf.

"I love you, Harry Langendorf," said Dolores Larson.

Harry Langendorf was ecstatic. He flew high into the heavens, higher than he had gone in a long time. He flew up above the clouds and soared gracefully down over the island.

The old were delighted. "It is such a pleasure to watch you fly," they said.

"It is such a pleasure to fly," said Harry Langendorf. "But it is a greater pleasure to know you and to be your friend."

For the next few days they explored their own island, found choice fishing spots, sailed along the coastline to become acquainted with the little villages on the sea, flew inland to watch the people working in the fields. They watched the huge flocks of cormorants black against the sky, saw the porpoises dancing on the water, watched the sun settle in splendor every evening and rise in white gold every morning.

Harry Langendorf had never been happier. He flew high above the clouds with some of the young. He dived with them swiftly towards the water and pulled out gracefully above the waves.

"Let's fly as high as we can," said one of the young.

"Not me," laughed Harry Langendorf, "I only fly as high as I want to. We have gone high enough for me."

They played for hours on end, chatted with the old pelicans on the shore, laughed about their flights and planned new and exciting trips in the weeks to come. Their new home was beautiful and the problems and quarrels of the former island seemed far away.

"You have led us to a paradise, Harry Langendorf," they said. "The young are happier than ever, the fish are fresh and sound, the scenery is glorious."

"And we are here together. We will have sad times and good times, tragedy and joy; whatever it is, we will have made it so."

The weeks passed happily. They took their flights along the coast as before. They explored and played, ate and rested, and chatted far into the night.

When they returned from one of their flights, an old pelican approached Harry Langendorf and said: "Maybe we should build our nests a little earlier this year, since there are no old nests to build on." They all agreed and the mating season began.

One day later in the spring, when the nests were being built and the fog was heavy on the island, Harry Langendorf complained of a sudden weariness. "I am very tired, Dolores Larson," he said. "I have never felt this way before."

"Maybe it will pass," she said, "when the fog lifts and the balmy air returns."

"No," said Harry Langendorf, "I do not think the sun will help this time. Something tells me I am going to die soon. I am old enough."

"I do not want you to die, Harry Langendorf," said Dolores Larson, "I love you too much."

"Will you fly with me to the reef of the dead?" he asked. "If it is to be my time to die I want to go there while I am still able to make the trip."

He paused to bid his friends good-bye.

"You will return to us soon, Harry Langendorf?" they asked.

"I do not know," he said. "I am very weary."

"Maybe you just need a good rest, some time alone with Dolores Larson. You have not had much time to yourself. We will keep the young ones busy building their nests."

Harry Langendorf smiled gently and wandered off with Dolores Larson. They flew north slowly and rested often. When they reached their former home, they flew around the island for remembrance sake. They saw the nest they had built together with love. He saw Samantha and Mary and the very first nest he had ever built. Then he flew with Dolores Larson to the reef of the dead.

The reef was covered with fog, as it often was. He found a perch on a flat rock where there was a place for both of them.

"I do not want you to stay with me to the end, Dolores Larson." he said. "Just stay for a few minutes. I will miss you so. I love you so. Maybe that's what death is—missing someone. But I want to die alone."

"I want to remain with you always," she said.

"Somehow you will," he said. "I love you Dolores Larson."

"If you die," she asked, "what will happen to you?"

"I do not know," he said.

"Do you want to die?"

"I don't think so," he replied, "But it is time."

"How can you be so calm, Harry Langendorf?"

"I do not know," he said. "But I am calm. I have enjoyed my life, flying along the shore, sitting quietly on the rocks for hours on end, feeling the wind lift me into the air, tasting the fresh fish, seeing the sun every day—and loving you, loving you so much."

"You could have done so much with another kind of mate, Harry Langendorf."

"What was there to do?" he asked.

"You could have gained back the leadership of the island."

"I did not want the leadership of the island," said Harry Langendorf. "I never really had it. Leadership is an illusion. I had good friends. That is enough."

"But I wanted to give you great things, Harry Langendorf. I wanted you to be proud of me."

"I love you, Dolores Larson, that is much more than being proud. I can see you, Dolores Larson, I can feel you."

"I am so sad to be losing you," she said.

"I am sad too," he answered. "But now you must go."

She looked at him and pecked affectionately at his pouch. She bowed gently and lifted her bill in love. "What shall I tell your friends, Harry Langendorf?"

"Tell them I have been very happy," he said. "And I am very grateful."

"Grateful to whom?" she asked.

"Just grateful," he said. "Now go, my love."

He watched her leave, the slow awkward takeoff he had learned to love, the skinny wings flapping against the wind, the stubby feet running across the waves. She flew over him one last time and lifted her bill. He lifted his bill in response and opened his pouch. He watched her until she was only a tiny speck in the hazy sunlight. Then she was gone.

He was alone on the reef of the dead. The fog was lifting late in the afternoon. The bleached bones surrounded him on the reef and he could see the gulls circling overhead. In the distance, the outline of a sailing ship moved south and on the horizon he could see the setting sun. He remembered a thousand suns he had seen settling over the ocean, the quiet hours on rocks, the trips along the coast, his mother and Charlie, Samantha Butterfield and Edward and Mary and, especially, Dolores Larson.

He looked at the sun a final time.

Harry Langendorf Pelican raised his head just a little.

"I have been very happy," he said.

"And I am grateful."

Then he died.

Pictorial Sources

The photographs on the following
pages were taken by David Siddon:
7, 10, 16, 17, 26, 27, 37, 38, 39, 40, 60,
61, 62, 83, 85, 89.

The photographs on pages 15 and 84
were taken by Joseph R. Jehl, Jr.